For a soft look, crochet this quick wrap holding one strand each of white and pastel yarns.

6

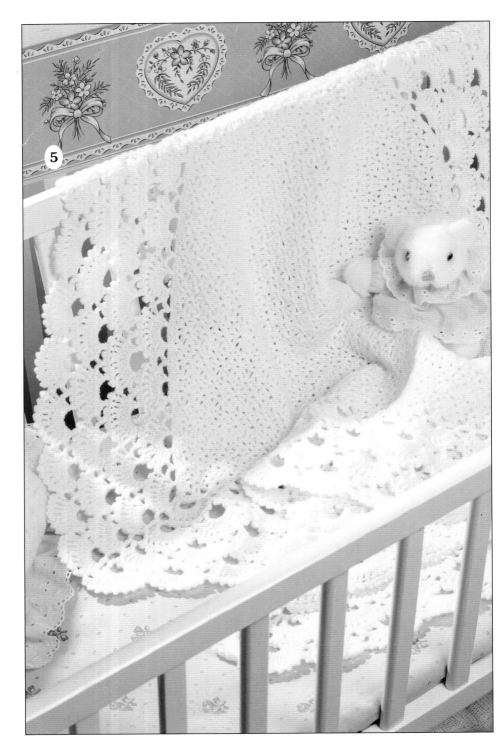

GENERAL INSTRUCTIONS

ABBREVIATIONS

ch(s)	chain(s)
dc	double crochet(s)
hdc	half double crochet(s)
K	knit
mm	millimeters
P	purl
PSSO	pass slipped stitch over
Rnd(s)	Round(s)
sc	single crochet(s)
sp(s)	space(s)
SSK	slip 2 sts as if to knit, knit together
st(s)	stitch(es)
tbl	through back loop(s)
tog	together
tr	treble crochet(s)
WYB	with yarn in back
WYF	with yarn in front
YO	yarn over

★ — work instructions following ★ as many **more** times as indicated in addition to the first time.

† to † — work all instructions from first † to second † **as many** times as specified.

( ) or [ ] — work enclosed instructions **as many** times as specified by the number immediately following **or** work all enclosed instructions in the stitch or space indicated **or** contains explanatory remarks.

colon (:) — the number(s) given after a colon at the end of a row or round denote(s) the number of stitches you should have on that row or round.

CROCHET TERMINOLOGY	
UNITED STATES	**INTERNATIONAL**
slip stitch (slip st) =	single crochet (sc)
single crochet (sc) =	double crochet (dc)
half double crochet (hdc) =	half treble crochet (htr)
double crochet (dc) =	treble crochet (tr)
treble crochet (tr) =	double treble crochet (dtr)
double treble crochet (dtr) =	triple treble crochet (ttr)
skip =	miss

KNIT TERMINOLOGY	
UNITED STATES	**INTERNATIONAL**
gauge =	tension
bind off =	cast off
yarn over (YO) =	yarn forward (yfwd) **or** yarn around needle (yrn)

GAUGE

Exact gauge is **essential** for proper size. Hook or needle size given in instructions is merely a guide and should never be used without first making a sample swatch approximately 4" square in the stitch, yarn, and hook or needle specified. Then measure it, counting your stitches and rows or rounds carefully. If your swatch is larger or smaller than specified, **make another, changing hook or needle size to get the correct gauge.** Keep trying until you find the size hook or needle that will give you the specified gauge.

ALUMINUM CROCHET HOOKS	
UNITED STATES	METRIC (mm)
B-1	2.25
C-2	2.75
D-3	3.25
E-4	3.50
F-5	3.75
G-6	4.00
H-8	5.00
I-9	5.50
J-10	6.00
K-10½	6.50
N	9.00
P	10.00
Q	15.00

We have made every effort to ensure that these instructions are accurate and complete. We cannot, however, be responsible for human error, typographical mistakes, or variations in individual work.

CROCHET BASICS

JOINING WITH SC

When instructed to join with sc, begin with a slip knot on hook. Insert hook in stitch or space indicated, YO and pull up a loop, YO and draw through both loops on hook.

CHANGING COLORS

Work the last stitch to within one step of completion, hook new yarn **(Fig. 1a or b)** and draw through all loops on hook. Cut old yarn and work over both ends.

Fig. 1a

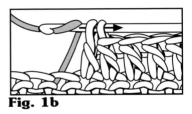

Fig. 1b

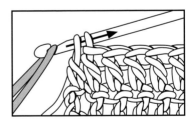

BACK LOOP ONLY

Work only in loop(s) indicated by arrow **(Fig. 2)**.

Fig. 2

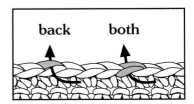

FREE LOOPS

After working in Back or Front Loops only on a row or round, there will be a ridge of unused loops. These are called the free loops. Later, when instructed to work in the free loops of the same row or round, work in these loops **(Fig. 3a)**.

When instructed to work in free loops of a chain, work in loop indicated by arrow **(Fig. 3b)**.

Fig. 3a

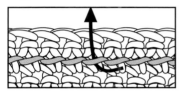

Fig. 3b

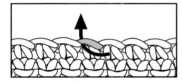

WHIPSTITCH

Place two Squares with **wrong** sides together. Beginning in center ch of first corner ch-3, sew through both pieces once to secure the beginning of the seam, leaving an ample yarn end to weave in later. Working through **both** loops of each stitch on **both** pieces, insert the needle from front to back through first stitch and pull yarn through **(Fig. 4)**, ★ insert the needle from front to back through next stitch and pull yarn through; repeat from ★ across ending in center ch of next corner ch-3.

Fig. 4

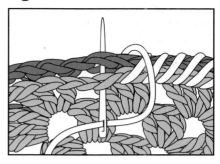

KNIT BASICS
YARN OVERS
(abbreviated YO)
After a knit stitch, before a knit stitch

Bring the yarn **forward** between the needles, then back **over** the top of the right hand needle, so that it is now in position to knit the next stitch **(Fig. 5a)**.

Fig. 5a

After a purl stitch, before a purl stitch

Take yarn **over** the right hand needle to the back, then forward **under** it, so that it is now in position to purl the next stitch **(Fig. 5b)**.

Fig. 5b

After a knit stitch, before a purl stitch

Bring yarn forward **between** the needles, then back **over** the top of the right hand needle and forward **between** the needles again, so that it is now in position to purl the next st *(Fig. 5c)*.

Fig. 5c

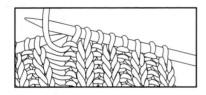

After a purl stitch, before a knit stitch

Take yarn **over** right hand needle to the back, so that it is now in position to knit the next stitch *(Fig. 5d)*.

Fig. 5d

KNIT 2 TOGETHER
(abbreviated K2 tog)

Insert the right needle into the **front** of the first two sts on the left needle as if to **knit** *(Fig. 6)*, then **knit** them together.

Fig. 6

PURL 2 TOGETHER
(abbreviated P2 tog)

Insert the right needle into the **front** of the first two sts on the left needle as if to **purl** *(Fig. 7)*, then **purl** them together.

Fig. 7

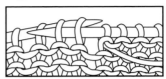

SLIP 1, KNIT 1, PASS SLIPPED STITCH OVER
(abbreviated slip 1, K1, PSSO)

Slip one st as if to **knit**. Knit the next st. With the left needle, bring the slipped st over the knit st *(Fig. 8)* and off the needle.

Fig. 8

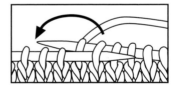

SLIP 1, KNIT 2, PASS SLIPPED STITCH OVER
(abbreviated slip 1, K2, PSSO)

Slip one stitch as if to **knit**. Knit the next two sts. With the left needle, bring the slipped st over the two knit sts *(Fig. 9)* and off the needle.

Fig. 9

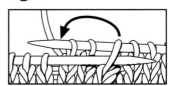

SLIP, SLIP, KNIT
(abbreviated SSK)

With yarn in back of work, separately slip two sts as if to **knit** *(Fig. 10a)*. Insert the **left** needle into the **front** of both slipped sts *(Fig. 10b)* and knit them together *(Fig. 10c)*.

Fig. 10a

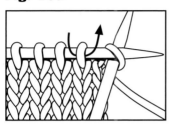

Fig. 10b

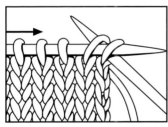

Fig. 10c

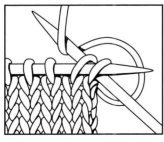

KNIT 3 TOGETHER
(abbreviated K3 tog)

Insert the right needle into the **front** of the first three sts on the left needle as if to **knit** *(Fig. 11)*, then knit them together.

Fig. 11

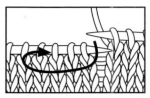

SLIP 1, KNIT 2 TOGETHER, PASS SLIPPED STITCH OVER
(abbreviated slip 1, K2 tog, PSSO)

Slip one st as if to **knit** *(Fig. 12a)*, then knit the next two sts together. With the left needle, bring the slipped st over the st just made *(Fig. 12b)* and off the needle.

Fig. 12a

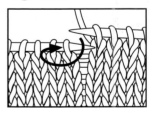

Fig. 12b

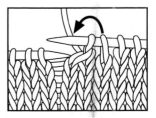

1. PRECIOUS AFGHAN
to knit

Shown on Back Cover.

Finished Size:
38" x 38"

MATERIALS

Baby Fingering Weight Yarn:
White - 6 ounces,
(170 grams, 860 yards)
Green - 4 ounces,
(110 grams, 575 yards)
Pink - 4 ounces,
(110 grams, 575 yards)
31" Circular knitting needle, size 8
(5.00 mm) **or** size needed for gauge
10" Straight knitting needles, size 8
(5.00 mm) **or** size needed for gauge
Yarn needle

GAUGE: In pattern,
24 sts and 24 rows = 4"

BLANKET

With White, cast on 199 sts
loosely.

Row 1: Purl across; drop White.

Note: When instructed to slip a
stitch throughout Blanket, always
hold the yarn to the **wrong** side and
slip as if to **purl**.

Row 2 (Right side)**:** With Green,
K3, (slip 1, K3) across.

Row 3: K3, (slip 1, K3) across;
drop Green.

Row 4: With White, K1, slip 1,
(K3, slip 1) across to last st, K1.

Row 5: P1, slip 1, (P3, slip 1)
across to last st, P1; drop White.

Rows 6 and 7: With Pink, repeat
Rows 2 and 3; at end of Row 7,
drop Pink.

Rows 8 and 9: Repeat Rows 4
and 5.

Repeat Rows 2-9 for pattern until
Blanket measures approximately
33" from cast on edge, ending by
working Row 7.

Cut Green and Pink.

With White, bind off all sts **loosely**.

EDGING

With White, cast on 8 sts **loosely**.

To work increase, knit into the
front **and** into the back of the next
st.

Row 1: K6, increase, WYF slip 1
as if to **purl**: 9 sts.

Row 2 (Right side)**:** K1 tbl **(Fig.
13)**, K1, ★ YO **(Fig. 5a, page
6)**, [slip 1 as if to **knit**, K1, PSSO
(Fig. 8, page 7)], K1; repeat from
★ once **more**, WYF slip 1 as if to
purl: 9 sts.

Fig. 13

Row 3: K1 tbl, K7, increase; **turn**, cast on 2 sts: 12 sts.

Row 4: K1, increase, K2, (YO, slip 1 as if to **knit**, K1, PSSO, K1) twice, YO, K1, WYF slip 1 as if to **purl**: 14 sts.

Row 5: K1 tbl, K 11, increase, WYF slip 1 as if to **purl**: 15 sts.

Row 6: K1 tbl, increase, K2, (YO, slip 1 as if to **knit**, K1, PSSO, K1) twice, YO, slip 1 as if to **knit**, K1, PSSO, K2, WYF slip 1 as if to **purl**: 16 sts.

Row 7: K1 tbl, K 13, K2 tog *(Fig. 6, page 7)*: 15 sts.

Row 8: Slip 1 as if to **purl**, K1, PSSO, slip 1 as if to **knit**, K1, PSSO, K4, (YO, slip 1 as if to **knit**, K1, PSSO, K1) twice, WYF slip 1 as if to **purl**: 13 sts.

Row 9: K1 tbl, K 10, K2 tog: 12 sts.

Row 10: Bind off 3 sts, K2, YO, slip 1 as if to **knit**, K1, PSSO, K1, YO, slip 1 as if to **knit**, K1, PSSO, WYF slip 1 as if to **purl**: 9 sts.

Repeat Rows 3-10 until Edging is long enough to fit around Blanket when slightly stretched plus 16 rows (2 points) for every corner, ending by working Row 10.

Bind off all sts **loosely**.

FINISHING
Sew ends together then sew straight edge of Edging to Blanket, pleating 16 rows at each corner.

Design by Tricia Gardella.

---

2. SWEETHEART AFGHAN
to knit

Shown on page 28.

Finished Size:
32" x 44"

MATERIALS
Sport Weight Yarn:
13 ounces,
(370 grams, 1,225 yards)
24" Circular knitting needle, size 7 (4.50 mm) **or** size needed for gauge

GAUGE: In Stockinette Stitch, 20 sts and 26 rows = 4"

AFGHAN
Cast on 150 sts.

Rows 1-10: Knit across.

To work increase, work into the front **and** into the back of the next st.

Row 11: K5, P 10, ★ increase, P 12; repeat from ★ across to last 5 sts, K5: 160 sts.

Row 12 (Right side)**:** Knit across.

Row 13: K5, purl across to last 5 sts, K5.

Rows 14-21: Repeat Rows 12 and 13, 4 times.

Row 22: K 27, YO *(Fig. 5a, page 6)*, SSK *(Figs. 10a-c, page 8)*, (K 33, YO, SSK) 3 times, K 26.

Row 23 AND ALL WRONG SIDE ROWS thru Row 53: K5, purl across to last 5 sts, K5.

Row 24: K 25, K2 tog *(Fig. 6, page 7)*, YO, K1 tbl *(Fig. 14)*, YO, SSK, (K 30, K2 tog, YO, K1 tbl, YO, SSK) 3 times, K 25.

Fig. 14

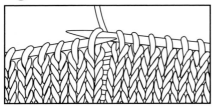

Row 26: K 24, K2 tog, YO, K1 tbl, (YO, SSK) twice, ★ K 28, K2 tog, YO, K1 tbl, (YO, SSK) twice; repeat from ★ 2 times **more**, K 24.

Row 28: K 23, (K2 tog, YO) twice, K1 tbl, (YO, SSK) twice, ★ K 26, (K2 tog, YO) twice, K1 tbl, (YO, SSK) twice; repeat from ★ 2 times **more**, K 23.

Row 30: K 22, (K2 tog, YO) twice, K1 tbl, (YO, SSK) 3 times, ★ K 24, (K2 tog, YO) twice, K1 tbl, (YO, SSK) 3 times; repeat from ★ 2 times **more**, K 22.

Row 32: K 21, (K2 tog, YO) 3 times, K1 tbl, (YO, SSK) 3 times, ★ K 22, (K2 tog, YO) 3 times, K1 tbl, (YO, SSK) 3 times; repeat from ★ 2 times **more**, K 21.

Row 34: K 20, ★ (K2 tog, YO) 3 times, K1 tbl, (YO, SSK) 4 times, K 20; repeat from ★ across.

Row 36: K 19, (K2 tog, YO) 4 times, K1 tbl, (YO, SSK) 4 times, ★ K 18, (K2 tog, YO) 4 times, K1 tbl, (YO, SSK) 4 times; repeat from ★ 2 times **more**, K 19.

Row 38: K 18, (K2 tog, YO) 4 times, K1 tbl, (YO, SSK) 5 times, ★ K 16, (K2 tog, YO) 4 times, K1 tbl, (YO, SSK) 5 times; repeat from ★ 2 times **more**, K 18.

Row 40: K 17, (K2 tog, YO) 3 times, K1 tbl, YO, SSK, YO, [slip 1, K2 tog, PSSO *(Figs. 12a & b, page 8)*], YO, K2 tog, YO, K1 tbl, (YO, SSK) 3 times, ★ K 14, (K2 tog, YO) 3 times, K1 tbl, YO, SSK, YO, slip 1, K2 tog, PSSO, YO, K2 tog, YO, K1 tbl, (YO, SSK) 3 times; repeat from ★ 2 times **more**, K 17.

Row 42: K 16, (K2 tog, YO) 3 times, K1 tbl, YO, SSK, YO, slip 1, K2 tog, PSSO, YO, (K2 tog, YO) twice, K1 tbl, (YO, SSK) 3 times, ★ K 12, (K2 tog, YO) 3 times, K1 tbl, YO, SSK, YO, slip 1, K2 tog, PSSO, YO, (K2 tog, YO) twice, K1 tbl, (YO, SSK) 3 times; repeat from ★ 2 times **more**, K 16.

Row 44: K 15, (K2 tog, YO) 3 times, K1 tbl, YO, (SSK, YO) twice, slip 1, K2 tog, PSSO, YO, (SSK, YO) twice, K1 tbl, (YO, SSK) 3 times, ★ K 10, (K2 tog, YO) 3 times, K1 tbl, YO, (SSK, YO) twice, slip 1, K2 tog, PSSO, YO, (SSK, YO) twice, K1 tbl, (YO, SSK) 3 times; repeat from ★ 2 times **more**, K 15.

Row 46: K 16, YO, (K2 tog, YO) twice, slip 1, K2 tog, PSSO, YO, (SSK, YO) twice, K1 tbl, YO, (K2 tog, YO) twice, slip 1, K2 tog, PSSO, YO, (SSK, YO) twice, ★ K 12, YO, (K2 tog, YO) twice, slip 1, K2 tog, PSSO, YO, (SSK, YO) twice, K1 tbl, YO, (K2 tog, YO) twice, slip 1, K2 tog, PSSO, YO, (SSK, YO) twice; repeat from ★ 2 times **more**, K 16.

Row 48: K 15, (SSK, YO) 3 times, K1 tbl, YO, (K2 tog, YO) twice, slip 1, K2 tog, PSSO, YO, (SSK, YO) twice, K1 tbl, (YO, K2 tog) 3 times, ★ K 10, (SSK, YO) 3 times, K1 tbl, YO, (K2 tog, YO) twice, slip 1, K2 tog, PSSO, YO, (SSK, YO) twice, K1 tbl, (YO, K2 tog) 3 times; repeat from ★ 2 times **more**, K 15.

Row 50: K 16, increase, (YO, SSK) twice, K3 tog *(Fig. 11, page 8)*, with left needle bring second st on right needle over first st and off the needle, YO, K2 tog, YO, increase, K1, increase, (YO, SSK) twice, K3 tog, with left needle bring second st on right needle over first st and off the needle, YO, K2 tog, YO, increase, ★ K 12, increase, (YO, SSK) twice, K3 tog, with left needle bring second st on right needle over first st and off the needle, YO, K2 tog, YO, increase, K1, increase, (YO, SSK) twice, K3 tog, with left needle bring second st on right needle over first st and off the needle, YO, K2 tog, YO, increase; repeat from ★ 2 times **more**, K 16.

Row 52: K 18, increase, YO, SSK, K3 tog, with left needle bring second st on right needle over first st and off the needle, YO, increase, K5, increase, YO, SSK, K3 tog, with left needle bring second st on right needle over first st and off the needle, YO, increase, ★ K 16, increase, YO, SSK, K3 tog, with left needle bring second st on right needle over first st and off the needle, YO, increase, K5, increase, YO, SSK, K3 tog, with left needle bring second st on right needle over first st and off the needle, YO, increase; repeat from ★ 2 times **more**, K 18.

Row 54: K 20, ★ WYB slip 3 sts as if to **purl**, WYF slip **same** 3 sts back onto left needle, WYB knit **same** 3 sts, K9, WYB slip 3 sts as if to **purl**, WYF slip **same** 3 sts back onto left needle, WYB knit **same** 3 sts, K 20; repeat from ★ across.

Row 55: K5, purl across to last 5 sts, K5.

Row 56: Knit across.

Rows 57-65: Repeat Rows 55 and 56, 4 times; then repeat Row 55 once **more**.

Rows 66-284: Repeat Rows 22-65, 4 times; then repeat Rows 22-64 once **more**.

Row 285: K5, P 10, ★ P2 tog *(Fig. 7, page 7)*, P 12; repeat from ★ across to last 5 sts, K5: 150 sts.

Rows 286-294: Knit across.

Bind off all sts in **knit**.

Design by Brooke Shellflower.

3. MARQUISE DIAMOND AFGHAN
to knit

Shown on page 1.

Finished Size:
31" x 42"

MATERIALS
Sport Weight Yarn:
21 ounces,
(600 grams, 1,980 yards)
24" Circular knitting needle, size 6
(4.25 mm) **or** size needed for gauge

GAUGE: In pattern,
28 sts and 36 rows = 4"

AFGHAN
Cast on 227 sts **loosely.**

Row 1 (Right side)**:** P2, ★ [slip 1, K2, PSSO *(Fig. 9, page 7)*], P2; repeat from ★ across: 182 sts.

Row 2: K2, ★ P1, YO *(Fig. 5b, page 6)*, P1, K2; repeat from ★ across: 227 sts.

Row 3: P2, (K3, P2) across.

Row 4: K2, (P3, K2) across.

Rows 5-12: Repeat Rows 1-4 twice.

Row 13: (P2, slip 1, K2, PSSO) twice, ★ (K3, P1) twice, K1, P1; repeat from ★ across to last 17 sts, K3, P1, K3, (slip 1, K2, PSSO, P2) twice: 223 sts.

Row 14: K2, P1, YO, P1, K2, P1, YO, P4, K1, P3, K1, P1, K1, ★ (P3, K1) twice, P1, K1; repeat from ★ across to last 15 sts, P3, K1, P4, YO, P1, K2, P1, YO, P1, K2: 227 sts.

Row 15: P2, K3, P2, K5, P1, K1, P1, ★ (K3, P1) twice, K1, P1; repeat from ★ across to last 12 sts, K5, P2, K3, P2.

Row 16: K2, P3, K2, P5, K1, P1, K1, ★ (P3, K1) twice, P1, K1; repeat from ★ across to last 12 sts, P5, K2, P3, K2.

Row 17: (P2, slip 1, K2, PSSO) twice, (K1, P1) 3 times, ★ (K2, P1) twice, (K1, P1) twice; repeat from ★ across to last 11 sts, K1, (slip 1, K2, PSSO, P2) twice: 223 sts.

Row 18: K2, P1, YO, P1, K2, P1, YO, P2, K1, (P1, K1) twice, ★ (P2, K1) twice, (P1, K1) twice; repeat from ★ across to last 9 sts, P2, YO, P1, K2, P1, YO, P1, K2: 227 sts.

Rows 19 and 20: Repeat Rows 15 and 16.

Rows 21 and 22: Repeat Rows 13 and 14.

Row 23: P2, K3, P2, K6, P1, ★ K2, P1, (K1, P1) twice, K2, P1; repeat from ★ across to last 13 sts, K6, P2, K3, P2.

Row 24: K2, P3, K2, P6, K1, ★ P2, K1, (P1, K1) twice, P2, K1; repeat from ★ across to last 13 sts, P6, K2, P3, K2.

Repeat Rows 13-24 for pattern until Afghan measures approx. 41", ending by working Row 16.

Last 12 Rows: Repeat Rows 1-4, 3 times.

Bind off all sts **loosely** in pattern.

Add Fringe across both ends as follows: Cut a piece of cardboard 6" wide and 9" long. Wind the yarn **loosely** and **evenly** around the cardboard lengthwise until the card is filled, then cut across one end; repeat as needed. Hold 6 strands of yarn together and fold in half. With **wrong** side of Afghan facing and using a crochet hook, draw the folded end up through a stitch and pull the loose ends through the folded end **(Fig. 15a)**; draw knot up **firmly (Fig. 15b)**. Repeat, working in every fourth stitch. Divide each group in half and knot together with half of next group **(Fig. 15c)**. Lay flat on hard surface and trim ends.

Design by Shobha Govindan.

Fig. 15a

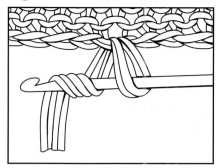

Fig. 15b

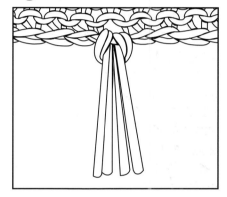

Fig. 15c

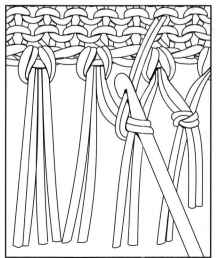

KNITTING NEEDLES		
UNITED STATES	ENGLISH U.K.	METRIC (mm)
0	13	2.00
1	12	2.25
2	11	2.75
3	10	3.25
4	9	3.50
5	8	3.75
6	7	4.00
7	6	4.50
8	5	5.00
9	4	5.50
10	3	6.00
10½	2	6.50
11	1	8.00
13	00	9.00
15	000	10.00
17	---	12.75

4. BABY BLUE AFGHAN
to crochet

Shown on page 29.

Finished Size:
35" x 46"

MATERIALS

Sport Weight Yarn:
Blue - 13 ounces,
(370 grams, 1,225 yards)
White - 9 ounces,
(260 grams, 850 yards)
Crochet hook, size G (4.00 mm) **or** size needed for gauge

GAUGE: One repeat from point to point and 11 rows = 5"

AFGHAN BODY

With Blue, ch 184 **loosely.**

Row 1 (Right side)**:** Dc in third ch from hook, ch 1, skip next ch, dc in next 10 chs, ch 1, (dc, ch 1) twice in next ch, dc in next 10 chs, ch 1, ★ (YO, skip next ch, insert hook in next ch, YO and pull up a loop, YO and draw through 2 loops on hook) twice, YO and draw through all 3 loops on hook, ch 1, skip next ch, dc in next 10 chs, ch 1, (dc, ch 1) twice in next ch, dc in next 10 chs, ch 1; repeat from ★ across to last 3 chs, YO, skip next ch, insert hook in next ch, YO and pull up a loop, YO and draw through 2 loops on hook, YO, insert hook in last ch, YO and pull up a loop, YO and draw through 2 loops on hook, YO and draw through all 3 loops on hook: 162 sts and 35 ch-1 sps.

Note: Loop a short piece of yarn around any stitch to mark last row as **right** side.

To work decrease (uses next 2 ch-1 sps), ★ YO, insert hook in **next** ch-1 sp, YO and pull up a loop, YO and draw through 2 loops on hook; repeat from ★ once **more**, YO and draw through all 3 loops on hook **(counts as one dc).**

To work ending decrease, YO, insert hook in next ch-1 sp, YO and pull up a loop, YO and draw through 2 loops on hook, YO, insert hook in last dc, YO and pull up a loop, YO and draw through 2 loops on hook, YO and draw through all 3 loops on hook **(counts as one dc).**

Rows 2-4: Ch 2, turn; dc in first ch-1 sp, ★ † ch 1, skip next dc, dc in next 9 dc and in next ch-1 sp, ch 1, (dc, ch 1) twice in next ch-1 sp, dc in next ch-1 sp and in next 9 dc, ch 1 †, decrease; repeat from ★ 5 times **more**, then repeat from † to † once, work ending decrease.

Finish off.

Row 5: With **right** side facing, join White with slip st in first dc; ch 2, dc in first ch-1 sp, ch 1, ★ † skip next 2 dc, dc in next dc, working around dc just made, dc in last skipped dc, (skip next dc, dc in next st, working around dc just made, dc in skipped dc) 5 times, ch 1, dc in next dc, working around dc just made, dc in ch before dc just worked into, skip next ch, (dc in next dc, working around dc just made, dc in skipped st, skip next dc) 5 times, ch 1 †, decrease, ch 1; repeat from ★ 5 times **more**, then repeat from † to † once, work ending decrease: 176 dc.

To work Puff St, ★ YO, insert hook in sp indicated, YO and pull up a loop even with loop on hook; repeat from ★ 2 times **more** (7 loops on hook), YO and draw through 6 loops on hook, YO and draw through remaining 2 loops on hook.

Row 6: Ch 2, turn; dc in first ch-1 sp, ★ † ch 1, skip next 2 dc, (work Puff St in sp **before** next dc, ch 1, skip next 2 dc) 5 times, work (Puff St, ch 3, Puff St) in next ch-1 sp, ch 1, skip next 2 dc, (work Puff St in sp **before** next dc, ch 1, skip next 2 dc) 5 times †, decrease; repeat from ★ 5 times **more**, then repeat from † to † once, work ending decrease: 84 Puff Sts.

Row 7: Ch 2, turn; dc in first ch-1 sp, ★ † ch 1, skip next 2 sts, dc in next Puff St, working around dc just

made, dc in skipped ch, (skip next ch, dc in next st, working around dc just made, dc in skipped ch) 5 times, ch 1, dc in next ch (third ch of ch-3), working around dc just made, dc in ch before ch just worked into (center ch of ch-3), skip next Puff St, (dc in next ch, working around dc just made, dc in skipped Puff St, skip next Puff St) 5 times, ch 1 †, decrease; repeat from ★ 5 times **more**, then repeat from † to † once, work ending decrease; finish off: 176 dc.

Row 8: With **right** side facing, join Blue with slip st in first dc; ch 2, dc in first ch-1 sp, ★ † ch 1, skip next dc, dc in next 10 dc, ch 1, skip next dc, (dc, ch 1) twice in next ch-1 sp, skip next dc, dc in next 10 dc, ch 1 †, decrease; repeat from ★ 5 times **more**, then repeat from † to † once, work ending decrease: 162 dc and 35 ch-1 sps.

Rows 9-102: Repeat Rows 2-8, 13 times; then repeat Rows 2-4 once **more**; do **not** finish off.

TOP EDGING
With Blue, ch 1, turn; slip st in first dc, (ch 1, slip st) in each ch-1 sp and in each dc across; finish off.

BOTTOM EDGING
With **right** side facing and working in free loops of beginning ch *(Fig. 3b, page 6)*, join Blue with slip st in first ch; (ch 1, slip st) in each ch and in each sp across; finish off.

Design by Jennine Korejko.

5. SIMPLY SHELLS AFGHAN
to crochet

Shown on page 3.

Finished Size:
32" x 44"

MATERIALS
Sport Weight Yarn:
15½ ounces,
(440 grams, 1,460 yards)
Crochet hook, size G (4.00 mm) **or**
size needed for gauge

GAUGE: In pattern,
3 Shells and 10 rows = 3¾"

AFGHAN BODY
To work Shell, dc in st or sp
indicated, (ch 1, dc) twice in same
st or sp.

Ch 113 **loosely.**

Row 1 (Right side)**:** Sc in second
ch from hook, skip next 2 chs, work
Shell in next ch, skip next 2 chs, sc
in next ch, ★ ch 3, sc in next ch,
skip next 2 chs, work Shell in next
ch, skip next 2 chs, sc in next ch;
repeat from ★ across: 16 Shells and
15 ch-3 sps.

Row 2: Ch 4 (**counts as first dc
plus ch 1, now and throughout),**
turn; (sc, ch 3, sc) in center dc of
next Shell, ★ work Shell in next
ch-3 sp, (sc, ch 3, sc) in center dc of
next Shell; repeat from ★ across to
last sc, ch 1, dc in last sc: 15 Shells
and 16 ch-3 sps.

Row 3: Ch 1, turn; sc in first dc,
work Shell in next ch-3 sp, ★ (sc,
ch 3, sc) in center dc of next Shell,
work Shell in next ch-3 sp; repeat
from ★ across to last dc, sc in last
dc: 16 Shells and 15 ch-3 sps.

Rows 4-85: Repeat Rows 2 and
3, 41 times.

Row 86: Ch 4, turn; sc in next
ch-1 sp, ch 2, sc in next ch-1 sp,
ch 1, ★ sc in next ch-3 sp, ch 1,
sc in next ch-1 sp, ch 2, sc in next
ch-1 sp, ch 1; repeat from ★ across
to last sc, dc in last sc; do **not** finish
off.

EDGING
Rnd 1: Ch 1, turn; 2 sc in first
dc, work 109 sc evenly spaced
across to last dc, 3 sc in last dc;
work 181 sc evenly spaced across
end of rows; working in free loops
of beginning ch *(Fig. 3b, page 6)*,
3 sc in first ch, work 109 sc evenly
spaced across to ch at base of last
sc, 3 sc in next ch; work 181 sc
evenly spaced across end of rows;
sc in same st as first sc; join with slip
st to first sc: 592 sc.

Rnd 2: Ch 8 **(counts as first dc plus ch 5, now and throughout)**, do **not** turn; skip next 3 sc, (sc in next sc, ch 5, skip next 3 sc) across to center sc of next corner 3-sc group, ★ (dc, ch 5) twice in center sc, skip next 3 sc, (sc in next sc, ch 5, skip next 3 sc) across to center sc of next corner 3-sc group; repeat from ★ 2 times **more**, dc in same st as first dc, ch 2, dc in first dc to form last loop: 152 loops.

Rnd 3: Ch 1, sc in same loop, 8 dc in next loop, (sc in next loop, ch 5, sc in next loop, 8 dc in next loop) across to next corner loop, ★ sc in corner loop, 8 dc in next loop, (sc in next loop, ch 5, sc in next loop, 8 dc in next loop) across to next corner loop; repeat from ★ 2 times **more**; join with slip st to first sc: 52 8-dc groups.

To work Picot, ch 3, slip st in top of dc just made.

Rnd 4: Slip st in first dc, ch 6, slip st in fourth ch from hook **(counts as first dc plus first Picot, now and throughout)**, dc in next dc, (work Picot, dc in next dc) 6 times, ★ † sc in next loop, dc in next dc, (work Picot, dc in next dc) 7 times †, repeat from † to † across to next corner sc, ch 5, skip corner sc, dc in next dc, (work Picot, dc in next dc) 7 times; repeat from ★ 2 times **more**, then repeat from † to † across, ch 2, dc in first dc to form last loop: 364 Picots.

Rnd 5: Ch 8, (skip next Picot, sc in next Picot, ch 5) 3 times, ★ † skip next 2 Picots, sc in next Picot, ch 5, (skip next Picot, sc in next Picot, ch 5) twice †, repeat from † to † across to next corner loop, (dc, ch 5) twice in corner loop, (skip next Picot, sc in next Picot, ch 5) 3 times; repeat from ★ 2 times **more**, then repeat from † to † across, dc in same loop as first dc, ch 2, dc in first dc to form last loop: 164 loops.

Rnds 6-12: Repeat Rnds 3-5 twice, then repeat Rnd 3 once **more**: 64 8-dc groups.

Rnd 13: Slip st in first dc, ch 6, slip st in fourth ch from hook, dc in next dc, (work Picot, dc in next dc) 6 times, ★ † sc in next loop, dc in next dc, (work Picot, dc in next dc) 7 times †, repeat from † to † across to next corner sc, ch 3, sc in third ch from hook, skip corner sc, dc in next dc, (work Picot, dc in next dc) 7 times; repeat from ★ 2 times **more**, then repeat from † to † across, ch 3, sc in third ch from hook; join with slip st to first dc, finish off.

Design by Terry Kimbrough.

6. RAINBOW DELIGHT AFGHAN
to crochet

Shown on page 2.

Finished Size:
36" x 39"

MATERIALS
Sport Weight Yarn:
White - 17 ounces,
(480 grams, 1,605 yards)
Pink - 2 ounces,
(60 grams, 190 yards)
Peach - 2 ounces,
(60 grams, 190 yards)
Yellow - 2 ounces,
(60 grams, 190 yards)
Green - 2 ounces,
(60 grams, 190 yards)
Blue - 2 ounces,
(60 grams, 190 yards)
Purple -1¹/₂ ounces,
(40 grams, 140 yards)
Crochet hook, size K (6.50 mm) **or**
size needed for gauge

Note: Afghan is worked holding two strands of yarn together throughout.

GAUGE: In pattern,
6 Clusters and 10 rows = 4"

AFGHAN BODY
Holding 2 strands of White together, ch 100 **loosely.**

Row 1 (Right side)**:** Sc in second ch from hook and in each ch across: 99 sc.

Note: Loop a short piece of yarn around any stitch to mark last row as **right** side.

Row 2: Ch 1, turn; sc in first sc, ★ ch 1, skip next sc, sc in next sc; repeat from ★ across; finish off: 49 ch-1 sps.

To work Cluster (uses one ch-1 sp), ★ YO, insert hook in ch-1 sp indicated, YO and pull up a loop, YO and draw through 2 loops on hook; repeat from ★ 2 times **more**, YO and draw through all 4 loops on hook.

Row 3: Holding one strand of White and one strand of Pink together and with **right** side facing, join yarn with slip st in first sc; ch 3 **(counts as first dc, now and throughout)**, work Cluster in next ch-1 sp, (ch 1, work Cluster in next ch-1 sp) across to last sc, dc in last sc: 49 Clusters and 48 ch-1 sps.

Row 4: Ch 1, turn; sc in first dc, ch 1, (sc in next ch-1 sp, ch 1) across to last dc, sc in last dc: 49 ch-1 sps.

Row 5: Ch 3, turn; work Cluster in next ch-1 sp, (ch 1, work Cluster in next ch-1 sp) across to last sc, dc in last sc.

Rows 6-8: Repeat Rows 4 and 5 once, then repeat Row 4 once **more**.

Finish off.

Row 9: Holding 2 strands of White together and with **right** side facing, join yarn with sc in first sc *(see Joining With Sc, page 5)*; sc in each ch-1 sp and in each sc across: 99 sc.

Row 10: Ch 1, turn; sc in first sc, ★ ch 1, skip next sc, sc in next sc; repeat from ★ across; finish off: 49 ch-1 sps.

Row 11: Holding one strand of White and one strand of Peach together and with **right** side facing, join yarn with slip st in first sc; ch 3, work Cluster in next ch-1 sp, (ch 1, work Cluster in next ch-1 sp) across to last sc, dc in last sc.

Rows 12-18: Repeat Rows 4-10.

Row 19: Holding one strand of White and one strand of Yellow together and with **right** side facing, join yarn with slip st in first sc; ch 3, work Cluster in next ch-1 sp, (ch 1, work Cluster in next ch-1 sp) across to last sc, dc in last sc.

Rows 20-26: Repeat Rows 4-10.

Row 27: Holding one strand of White and one strand of Green together and with **right** side facing, join yarn with slip st in first sc; ch 3, work Cluster in next ch-1 sp, (ch 1, work Cluster in next ch-1 sp) across to last sc, dc in last sc.

Rows 28-34: Repeat Rows 4-10.

Row 35: Holding one strand of White and one strand of Blue together and with **right** side facing, join yarn with slip st in first sc; ch 3, work Cluster in next ch-1 sp, (ch 1, work Cluster in next ch-1 sp) across to last sc, dc in last sc.

Rows 36-42: Repeat Rows 4-10.

Row 43: Holding one strand of White and one strand of Purple together and with **right** side facing, join yarn with slip st in first sc; ch 3, work Cluster in next ch-1 sp, (ch 1, work Cluster in next ch-1 sp) across to last sc, dc in last sc.

Rows 44-50: Repeat Rows 4-10.

Rows 51-87: Repeat Rows 3-35 once, then repeat Rows 4-7 once **more**.

Finish off.

Row 88: Holding 2 strands of White together and with **wrong** side facing, join yarn with sc in first dc; ch 1, (sc in next ch-1 sp, ch 1) across to last dc, sc in last dc: 49 ch-1 sps.

Row 89: Ch 1, turn; sc in each sc and in each ch-1 sp across; do **not** finish off: 99 sc.

EDGING

Rnd 1: Ch 1, do **not** turn; work 115 sc evenly spaced across end of rows; working in free loops of beginning ch *(Fig. 3b, page 6)*, 3 sc in first ch, sc in next 97 chs, 3 sc in next ch; work 115 sc evenly spaced across end of rows; working across Row 89, 3 sc in first sc, sc in each sc across to last sc, 3 sc in last sc; join with slip st to Back Loop Only of first sc *(Fig. 2, page 5)*: 436 sc.

Rnd 2: Ch 1, working in Back Loops Only, sc in same st and in each sc across to center sc of next corner, 3 sc in corner sc, ★ sc in each sc across to center sc of next corner, 3 sc in corner sc; repeat from ★ 2 times **more**, sc in last sc; join with slip st to **both** loops of first sc: 444 sc.

To work Puff St, ★ YO, insert hook in st indicated, YO and pull up a loop even with loop on hook; repeat from ★ once **more**, YO and draw through all 5 loops on hook.

Rnd 3: Pull up a ½" loop, working in both loops, work Puff St in same st, ch 3, work Puff St in third ch from hook and in same st as first Puff St, skip next 2 sc, ★ (work Puff St in next sc, ch 3, work Puff St in third ch from hook and in same st as first Puff St, skip next 2 sc) across to center sc of next corner, work Puff St in corner sc, (ch 3, work Puff St in third ch from hook and in same st as first Puff St) twice, skip next 2 sc; repeat from ★ around; join with slip st to top of first Puff St, finish off.

Design by C. A. Riley.

---

7. NAPTIME GRANNY AFGHAN
to crochet

Shown on page 30.

Finished Size:
37" x 42"

MATERIALS
Sport Weight Yarn:
White - 16 ounces,
(450 grams, 1,280 yards)
Blue - 4¼ ounces,
(120 grams, 340 yards)
Pink - 4 ounces,
(110 grams, 320 yards)
Crochet hook, size G (4.00 mm) **or** size needed for gauge
Yarn needle

GAUGE: Each Square = 2¼"
Each Strip = 5"w

STRIP A (Make 4)
SQUARE (Make 68)
Note: Each Strip consists of 17 Squares.

Rnd 1 (Right side)**:** With Pink, ch 4, 2 dc in fourth ch from hook, ch 3, (3 dc in same ch, ch 3) 3 times; join with slip st to top of beginning ch-4, finish off: 4 ch-3 sps.

Note: Loop a short piece of yarn around any stitch to mark last round as **right** side.

Rnd 2: With **right** side facing, join White with slip st in any ch-3 sp; ch 3 **(counts as first dc, now and throughout)**, (2 dc, ch 3, 3 dc) in same sp, ch 1, ★ (3 dc, ch 3, 3 dc) in next ch-3 sp, ch 1; repeat from ★ 2 times **more**; join with slip st to first dc, finish off: 24 dc and 8 sps.

With White, whipstitch Squares together forming 4 vertical strips of 17 Squares each **(Fig. 4, page 6)**, beginning in center ch of first corner and ending in center ch of next corner.

EDGING
Rnd 1: With **right** side of short edge facing, join White with sc in right corner ch-3 sp **(see Joining With Sc, page 5)**; ch 3, sc in same sp, † ch 1, skip next dc, sc in next dc, ch 1, sc in next ch-1 sp, ch 1, skip next dc, sc in next dc, ch 1, (sc, ch 3, sc) in next corner ch-3 sp, ch 1, skip next dc, sc in next dc, ch 1, sc in next ch-1 sp, ch 1, skip next dc, sc in next dc, ch 1, [(sc in next sp, ch 1) twice, skip next dc, sc in next dc, ch 1, sc in next ch-1 sp, ch 1, skip next dc, sc in next dc, ch 1] across to next corner ch-3 sp †, (sc, ch 3, sc) in corner ch-3 sp, repeat from † to † once; join with slip st to first sc: 180 sps.

Rnd 2: Ch 1, (sc, ch 3, sc) in first corner ch-3 sp, ch 1, (sc in next ch-1 sp, ch 1) across to next corner ch-3 sp, ★ (sc, ch 3, sc) in corner ch-3 sp, ch 1, (sc in next ch-1 sp, ch 1) across to next corner ch-3 sp; repeat from ★ 2 times **more**; join with slip st to first sc, finish off: 184 sps.

Rnd 3: With **right** side facing, join Blue with slip st in any corner ch-3 sp; ch 3, (2 dc, ch 3, 3 dc) in same sp, ch 1, skip next ch-1 sp, (3 dc in next ch-1 sp, ch 1, skip next ch-1 sp) across to next corner ch-3 sp, ★ (3 dc, ch 3, 3 dc) in corner ch-3 sp, ch 1, skip next ch-1 sp, (3 dc in next ch-1 sp, ch 1, skip next ch-1 sp) across to next corner ch-3 sp; repeat from ★ 2 times **more**; join with slip st to first dc, finish off: 288 dc and 96 sps.

Rnd 4: With **right** side facing, join White with slip st in any corner ch-3 sp; ch 3, (2 dc, ch 3, 3 dc) in same sp, ch 1, (3 dc in next ch-1 sp, ch 1) across to next corner ch-3 sp, ★ (3 dc, ch 3, 3 dc) in corner ch-3 sp, ch 1, (3 dc in next ch-1 sp, ch 1) across to next corner ch-3 sp; repeat from ★ 2 times **more**; join with slip st to first dc, finish off: 300 dc and 100 sps.

STRIP B (Make 3)
SQUARE (Make 51)
Note: Each Strip consists of 17 Squares.

Rnd 1 (Right side)**:** With Blue, ch 4, 2 dc in fourth ch from hook, ch 3, (3 dc in same ch, ch 3) 3 times; join with slip st to top of beginning ch-4, finish off: 4 ch-3 sps.

Note: Mark last round as **right** side.

Rnd 2: With **right** side facing, join White with slip st in any ch-3 sp; ch 3, (2 dc, ch 3, 3 dc) in same sp, ch 1, ★ (3 dc, ch 3, 3 dc) in next ch-3 sp, ch 1; repeat from ★ 2 times **more**; join with slip st to first dc, finish off: 24 dc and 8 sps.

With White, whipstitch Squares together forming 3 vertical strips of 17 Squares each, beginning in center ch of first corner and ending in center ch of next corner.

EDGING

Rnds 1 and 2: Work same as Strip A: 184 sps.

Rnd 3: With **right** side facing, join Pink with slip st in any corner ch-3 sp; ch 3, (2 dc, ch 3, 3 dc) in same sp, ch 1, skip next ch-1 sp, (3 dc in next ch-1 sp, ch 1, skip next ch-1 sp) across to next corner ch-3 sp, ★ (3 dc, ch 3, 3 dc) in corner ch-3 sp, ch 1, skip next ch-1 sp, (3 dc in next ch-1 sp, ch 1, skip next ch-1 sp) across to next corner ch-3 sp; repeat from ★ 2 times **more**; join with slip st to first dc, finish off: 288 dc and 96 sps.

Rnd 4: With **right** side facing, join White with slip st in any corner ch-3 sp; ch 3, (2 dc, ch 3, 3 dc) in same sp, ch 1, (3 dc in next ch-1 sp, ch 1) across to next corner ch-3 sp, ★ (3 dc, ch 3, 3 dc) in corner ch-3 sp, ch 1, (3 dc in next ch-1 sp, ch 1) across to next corner ch-3 sp; repeat from ★ 2 times **more**; join with slip st to first dc, finish off: 300 dc and 100 sps.

ASSEMBLY

With White, whipstitch Strips together in the following sequence, beginning in the center ch of first corner and ending in center ch of next corner: Strip A, (Strip B, Strip A) 3 times.

BORDER

Rnd 1: With **right** side of short edge facing, join White with sc in right corner ch-3 sp; ch 3, sc in same sp, † ch 1, skip next dc, sc in next dc, ch 1, (sc in next ch-1 sp, ch 1, skip next dc, sc in next dc, ch 1) 4 times, [(sc in next sp, ch 1) twice, skip next dc, sc in next dc, ch 1, (sc in next ch-1 sp, ch 1, skip next dc, sc in next dc, ch 1) 4 times] across to next corner ch-3 sp, (sc, ch 3, sc) in corner ch-3 sp, ch 1, skip next dc, sc in next dc, ch 1, (sc in next ch-1 sp, ch 1, skip next dc, sc in next dc, ch 1) across to next corner ch-3 sp †, (sc, ch 3, sc) in corner ch-3 sp, repeat from † to † once; join with slip st to first sc: 336 sps.

Rnd 2: Ch 1, (sc, ch 3, sc) in first corner ch-3 sp, ch 1, (sc in next ch-1 sp, ch 1) across to next corner ch-3 sp, ★ (sc, ch 3, sc) in corner ch-3 sp, ch 1, (sc in next ch-1 sp, ch 1) across to next corner ch-3 sp; repeat from ★ 2 times **more**; join with slip st to first sc: 340 sps.

To work Cluster *(uses one ch-3 sp)* ★ YO, insert hook in ch-3 sp indicated, YO and pull up a loop, YO and draw through 2 loops on hook; repeat from ★ once **more**, YO and draw through all 3 loops on hook.

To work Scallop, ch 3, dc in third ch from hook.

Rnd 3: (Slip st, ch 2, work Cluster, ch 2, slip st) in first corner ch-3 sp, work Scallop, skip next ch-1 sp, (slip st in next ch-1 sp, work Scallop, skip next ch-1 sp) across to next corner ch-3 sp, ★ (slip st, ch 2, work Cluster, ch 2, slip st) in corner ch-3 sp, work Scallop, skip next ch-1 sp, (slip st in next ch-1 sp, work Scallop, skip next ch-1 sp) across to next corner ch-3 sp; repeat from ★ 2 times **more**; join with slip st to first slip st, finish off.

Design by Anne Halliday.

8. DREAMY HEARTS AFGHAN
to crochet

Shown on Front Cover.

Finished Size:
41½" x 52"

MATERIALS
Sport Weight Yarn:
White - 27 ounces,
(770 grams, 2,160 yards)
Blue - 5 ounces,
(140 grams, 400 yards)
Pink - 5 ounces,
(140 grams, 400 yards)
Green - 5 ounces,
(140 grams, 400 yards)
Yellow - 5 ounces,
(140 grams, 400 yards)
Crochet hook, size G (4.00 mm) **or**
size needed for gauge
Yarn needle

GAUGE:
Each Heart Square = 4¼"
Each Large Square = 10½"

HEART SQUARES A-D
Referring to the table below, make
12 of **each** Square in the colors
indicated.

	Rnds 1-3	Rnds 4 & 5
A	Yellow	White
B	Green	White
C	Blue	White
D	Pink	White

To work treble crochet
(abbreviated *tr*), YO twice, insert
hook in st indicated, YO and pull
up a loop (4 loops on hook), (YO
and draw through 2 loops on hook)
3 times.

With color indicated, ch 8 **loosely**.

Rnd 1 (Right side)**:** 3 Tr in fourth
ch from hook, tr in next ch, dc in
next ch, hdc in next ch, 3 sc in
last ch; working in free loops of
beginning ch **(Fig. 3b, page 6)**,
hdc in next ch, dc in next ch, tr in
next ch, (3 tr, ch 3, slip st) in same
ch as first tr; do **not** join: 16 sts and
2 ch-3 sps.

Note: Loop a short piece of yarn
around any stitch to mark last round
as **right** side.

Rnd 2: Ch 1, sc in same ch as
last slip st, ch 1, dc in next ch-3 sp,
ch 1, place marker around ch-1 just
made for st placement, (tr, ch 1) 4
times in next tr, tr in next tr, ch 1,
skip next tr, (dc in next st, ch 1, skip
next st) twice, (dc, ch 4, dc) in next
sc, ch 1, skip next sc, (dc in next st,
ch 1, skip next st) twice, tr in next
tr, ch 1, (tr, ch 1) 4 times in next tr,
dc in last ch-3 sp, ch 1; join with slip
st to first sc: 19 sts and 19 sps.

To work Picot, ch 3, dc in third ch
from hook.

Rnd 3: Ch 1, **turn**; skip first ch-1 sp, slip st in next dc, work Picot, (skip next ch-1 sp, slip st in next st, work Picot) 7 times, (slip st, work Picot) twice in next ch-4 sp, skip next dc, slip st in next dc, (work Picot, skip next ch-1 sp, slip st in next st) 7 times, ch 1; join with slip st to same st as previous joining, finish off: 17 Picots.

Rnd 4: With **wrong** side facing and working in **front** of Picot, join White with sc in marked ch-1 sp on Rnd 2 *(see Joining With Sc, page 5)*; ch 6, working in **front** of next Picot, sc in skipped ch-1 sp on Rnd 2, ch 4 **(counts as first dc plus ch 1), turn**; (3 dc, ch 3, 3 dc) in next ch-6 sp, ch 1, dc in next sc, ch 1, working **behind** Picots and in skipped ch-1 sps on Rnd 2, (sc in next ch-1 sp, ch 1) twice, (dc, ch 3, dc) in next ch-1 sp, ch 1, hdc in next ch-1 sp, ch 1, sc in next ch-1 sp, (ch 1, slip st in next ch-1 sp) twice, ch 2, skip next slip st, (slip st, ch 2) twice in sp **before** next slip st, (slip st in next ch-1 sp, ch 1) twice, sc in next ch-1 sp, ch 1, hdc in next ch-1 sp, ch 1, (dc, ch 3, dc) in next ch-1 sp, ch 1, (sc in next ch-1 sp, ch 1) twice; join with slip st to first dc: 26 sts and 22 sps along outer edge.

Rnd 5: Do **not** turn; slip st in first ch-1 sp, ch 3 **(counts as first dc, now and throughout)**, 2 dc in same sp, ch 1, (3 dc, ch 3, 3 dc) in next ch-3 sp, ch 1, (3 dc in next ch-1 sp, ch 1, skip next ch-1 sp) twice, (3 dc, ch 3, 3 dc) in next ch-3 sp, ch 1, skip next ch-1 sp, (3 dc in next ch-1 sp, ch 1, skip next sp) twice, 2 dc in next slip st, (dc, ch 3, dc) in next ch-2 sp, 2 dc in next slip st, ch 1, skip next ch-2 sp, (3 dc in next ch-1 sp, ch 1, skip next ch-1 sp) twice, (3 dc, ch 3, 3 dc) in next ch-3 sp, ch 1, skip next ch-1 sp, 3 dc in next ch-1 sp, ch 1, skip last ch-1 sp; join with slip st to first dc, finish off: 48 dc and 16 sps.

LARGE SQUARES

With White and using Assembly Diagram as a guide for placement, whipstitch 4 Heart Squares together forming one Large Square *(Fig. 4, page 6)*.

ASSEMBLY DIAGRAM

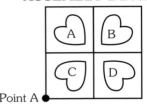

Point A

BORDER

Rnd 1: With **right** side facing, join White with sc in ch-3 sp at Point A; ch 3, sc in same sp, ★ † ch 1, skip next dc, sc in next dc, ch 1, (sc in next ch-1 sp, ch 1, skip next dc, sc in next dc, ch 1) 3 times, (sc in next sp, ch 1) twice, skip next dc, sc in next dc, ch 1, (sc in next ch-1 sp, ch 1, skip next dc, sc in next dc, ch 1) 3 times †, (sc, ch 3, sc) in next ch-3 sp; repeat from ★ 2 times **more**, then repeat from † to † once; join with slip st to first sc, finish off: 72 sc and 72 sps.

Rnd 2: With **right** side facing, join Yellow with slip st in first ch-3 sp; ch 3, 2 dc in same sp, ch 1, skip next ch-1 sp, (3 dc in next ch-1 sp, ch 1, skip next ch-1 sp) 8 times, 3 dc in next ch-3 sp changing to Blue in last dc made *(Fig. 1a, page 5)*, ch 3, 3 dc in same sp, ch 1, skip next ch-1 sp, (3 dc in next ch-1 sp, ch 1, skip next ch-1 sp) 8 times, 3 dc in next ch-3 sp changing to Pink in last dc made, ch 3, 3 dc in same sp, ch 1, skip next ch-1 sp, (3 dc in next ch-1 sp, ch 1, skip next ch-1 sp) 8 times, 3 dc in next ch-3 sp changing to Green in last dc made, ch 3, 3 dc in same sp, ch 1, skip next ch-1 sp, (3 dc in next ch-1 sp, ch 1, skip next ch-1 sp) 8 times, 3 dc in same sp as first dc, ch 3; join with slip st to first dc, finish off: 120 dc and 40 sps.

Rnd 3: With **right** side facing, join White with slip st in any corner ch-3 sp; ch 3, (2 dc, ch 3, 3 dc) in same sp, ch 1, (3 dc in next ch-1 sp, ch 1) across to next corner ch-3 sp, ★ (3 dc, ch 3, 3 dc) in corner ch-3 sp, ch 1, (3 dc in next ch-1 sp, ch 1) across to next corner ch-3 sp; repeat from ★ 2 times **more**; join with slip st to first dc, finish off: 132 dc and 44 sps.

ASSEMBLY

With White and using Placement Diagram as a guide, whipstitch Large Squares together forming 3 vertical strips of 4 Large Squares each; then whipstitch strips together.

PLACEMENT DIAGRAM

EDGING

Rnd 1: With **right** side facing, join White with sc in any corner ch-3 sp; ch 2, sc in same sp, ★ † ch 1, skip next dc, sc in next dc, ch 1, (sc in next ch-1 sp, ch 1, skip next dc, sc in next dc, ch 1) 10 times, [(sc in next sp, ch 1) twice, skip next dc, sc in next dc, ch 1, (sc in next ch-1 sp, ch 1, skip next dc, sc in next dc, ch 1) 10 times] across to next corner ch-3 sp †, (sc, ch 2, sc) in corner ch-3 sp; repeat from ★ 2 times **more**, then repeat from † to † once; join with slip st to first sc: 322 sc and 322 sps.

Rnd 2: Slip st in first corner ch-2 sp, ch 1, (sc, ch 2, sc) in same sp, ch 1, (sc in next ch-1 sp, ch 1) across to next corner ch-2 sp, ★ (sc, ch 2, sc) in corner ch-2 sp, ch 1, (sc in next ch-1 sp, ch 1) across to next corner ch-2 sp; repeat from ★ 2 times **more**; join with slip st to first sc: 326 sc and 326 sps.

Rnd 3: Slip st in first corner ch-2 sp, ch 6, dc in same sp, ch 2, (dc in next ch-1 sp, ch 2) across to next corner ch-2 sp, ★ (dc, ch 3, dc) in corner ch-2 sp, ch 2, (dc in next ch-1 sp, ch 2) across to next corner ch-2 sp; repeat from ★ 2 times **more**; join with slip st to third ch of beginning ch-6.

Rnd 4: Slip st in first corner ch-3 sp, ch 3, (2 dc, ch 3, 3 dc) in same sp, ch 1, (3 dc in next ch-2 sp, ch 1) across to next corner ch-3 sp, ★ (3 dc, ch 3, 3 dc) in corner ch-3 sp, ch 1, (3 dc in next ch-2 sp, ch 1) across to next corner ch-3 sp; repeat from ★ 2 times **more**; join with slip st to first dc, finish off.

Rnd 5: With **right** side facing, join Blue with slip st in any corner ch-3 sp; ch 3, (2 dc, ch 3, 3 dc) in same sp, ch 1, (3 dc in next ch-1 sp, ch 1) across to next corner ch-3 sp, ★ (3 dc, ch 3, 3 dc) in corner ch-3 sp, ch 1, (3 dc in next ch-1 sp, ch 1) across to next corner ch-3 sp; repeat from ★ 2 times **more**; join with slip st to first dc, finish off.

Rnd 6: With Yellow, repeat Rnd 5.

Rnd 7: With Green, repeat Rnd 5.

Rnd 8: With Pink, repeat Rnd 5.

Rnd 9: With White, repeat Rnd 5; do **not** finish off.

Rnd 10: Slip st in next 2 dc and in next corner ch-3 sp, ch 1, [(dc, ch 1) twice, slip st] in same sp, ch 1, skip next dc, (dc, ch 1) twice in next dc, [slip st in next ch-1 sp, ch 1, skip next dc, (dc, ch 1) twice in next dc] across to next corner ch-3 sp, ★ slip st in corner ch-3 sp, ch 1, [(dc, ch 1) twice, slip st] in same sp, ch 1, skip next dc, (dc, ch 1) twice in next dc, [slip st in next ch-1 sp, ch 1, skip next st, (dc, ch 1) twice in next st] across to next corner ch-3 sp; repeat from ★ 2 times **more**; join with slip st at base of beginning ch-1, finish off.

RUFFLE

Rnd 1: With **right** side facing, working in **front** of Edging and in unworked sc on Rnd 2 of Edging, join White with sc in first sc to left of any corner ch-3 sp; (ch 2, sc in next sc) across to next corner ch-3 sp, ★ ch 3, skip corner ch-3 sp, sc in next sc, (ch 2, sc in next sc) across to next corner ch-3 sp; repeat from ★ 2 times **more**, dc in first sc to form last ch-3 sp: 326 sc and 326 sps.

Rnd 2: Ch 5, (dc in same sp, ch 2) 7 times, (dc, ch 2) 4 times in each ch-2 sp across to next corner ch-3 sp, ★ (dc, ch 2) 8 times in corner ch-3 sp, (dc, ch 2) 4 times in each ch-2 sp across to next corner ch-3 sp; repeat from ★ 2 times **more**; join with slip st to third ch of beginning ch-5, finish off.

Design by Anne Halliday.